Pakistan TourGuide

What is this country about

TABLE OF CONTENT

Introduction

- Chapter 1: Discovering Pakistan: An Overview
- Chapter 2: Punjab – The Heart of Pakistan
- Chapter 3: Sindh – The Land of Sufis
- Chapter 4: Khyber Pakhtunkhwa – The Frontier Province
- Chapter 5: Balochistan – The Land of Mysteries
- Chapter 6: Gilgit-Baltistan – The Mountain Paradise
- Chapter 7: Azad Kashmir – The Valley of Paradise
- Chapter 8: Karachi – The City of Lights
- Chapter 9: Lahore – The Cultural Capital
- Chapter 10: Islamabad – The Modern Capital
- Chapter 11: Peshawar – The Gateway to Central Asia
- Chapter 12: The Majestic Mountains of Pakistan
- Chapter 13: The Rivers and Lakes of Pakistan
- Chapter 14: The Deserts of Pakistan
- Chapter 15: Pakistan's Great Monuments
- Chapter 16: Festivals and Celebrations
- Chapter 17: The Diverse Cuisine of Pakistan
- Chapter 18: Arts and Crafts of Pakistan
- Chapter 19: Practical Travel Information
- Chapter 20: Off the Beaten Path – Hidden Gems of Pakistan
- Chapter 21: The Future of Tourism in Pakistan

Before we start..

Welcome to What is this country about..
Whether you're planning your first trip or you've visited before, this book is here to be your trusty travel companion. Pakistan is a land of incredible diversity—from the towering peaks of the north to the bustling markets of its cities, from ancient history etched in stone to the warm hospitality that greets you everywhere. This guide is crafted with love and a deep understanding of what makes Pakistan tick, and it's packed with insights that go beyond the usual tourist spots.

We'll take you on a journey through Pakistan's vibrant cities like Karachi and Lahore, where tradition and modernity coexist in the most fascinating ways. You'll get the lowdown on where to find the best street food, the hidden historical gems, and the cultural nuances that make each region unique. We're talking about everything from the poetic soul of Lahore to the rugged beauty of Balochistan.

If you're into adventure, you're in for a treat. Pakistan's northern regions are a playground for trekkers and mountaineers, with some of the world's highest peaks and most breathtaking landscapes. But even if you're not the outdoorsy type, there's plenty here for you—think scenic drives, serene lakes, and ancient fortresses that tell tales of empires long gone.

This book is more than just a list of places to go—it's about how to experience Pakistan like a local. So, whether you're sipping chai in a roadside dhaba or hiking through the meadows of Hunza, this guide has got you covered. Let's explore Pakistan together, one chapter at a time.

PART 1

Introduction

Chapter 1: Discovering Pakistan: An Overview

A Land of Layers: Unpacking Pakistan's History

Welcome to Pakistan—a land where history isn't just something you read about in books; it's something you feel in the air, see in the architecture, and taste in the food. Pakistan's history is a rich tapestry woven with the threads of ancient civilizations, religious conquests, and colonial rule.

From the ruins of Mohenjo-Daro, one of the world's earliest urban centers, to the Mughal-era splendors of Lahore, every corner of this country tells a story.
Let's start with the Indus Valley Civilization, one of the oldest in the world, which laid the foundations of urban planning, trade, and culture as early as 2500 BCE. Fast forward to the arrival of Islam in the 7th century, and you'll see how it shaped the region's identity, leading to the grandeur of the Mughal Empire.

The British colonial period added another layer, bringing with it railways, tea culture, and a new wave of architectural styles. Each era left its mark, making Pakistan a complex mosaic of influences.
When you travel through Pakistan, you're not just moving from one location to another; you're moving through time.

The country's history isn't confined to museums—it's alive in the forts, mosques, and even the everyday lives of its people. Expect to encounter a country that holds its history close, yet wears it lightly.

Geography: More Than Just Mountains

When people think of Pakistan, they often picture the towering peaks of the Karakoram, home to K2, the second-highest mountain in the world. But Pakistan's geography is as diverse as it is dramatic. Stretching from the Arabian Sea in the south to the high-altitude plains of the north, Pakistan's terrain includes deserts, forests, rivers, and coastlines—all within its borders.

Let's break it down:
The North: Beyond the mountains, the northern areas are a haven for trekkers and nature lovers. You'll find lush valleys like Hunza and Swat, each offering a different flavor of paradise. The north isn't just about natural beauty; it's also home to ancient trade routes like the Silk Road, adding a historical depth to your travels.

The Punjab
Moving south, the Punjab region is the agricultural heartland, where green fields stretch as far as the eye can see. It's also the cultural hub, with Lahore standing as its vibrant soul. Expect to find a mix of Mughal grandeur, colonial elegance, and a modern urban buzz.

Sindh
Down in Sindh, history blends seamlessly with daily life. Karachi, the country's largest city, is a melting pot of cultures, offering a taste of everything from spicy street food to high-end dining, from ancient sites like Thatta to the modern hustle of a global port city.

Balochistan
The largest but least populated province, Balochistan, is a rugged, untamed land of deserts, mountains, and coastline. This is where you go when you want to get off the beaten path. It's raw, it's remote, and it's incredibly rewarding.

Each region offers a distinct experience, so whether you're into history, nature, or urban exploration, Pakistan's geography has something for you.

Cultural Diversity: A Symphony of Traditions

One of Pakistan's most compelling features is its cultural diversity. With over 70 languages spoken and a multitude of ethnic groups, Pakistan is a country where traditions vary as widely as the landscape. The people of Pakistan are known for their hospitality—expect to be offered tea, snacks, or even a meal at almost every stop.
Punjabis: Known for their lively spirit and love for food, Punjabis are the life of any gathering.
Expect to see vibrant festivals, hear bhangra music, and taste some of the richest food you've ever had.
Sindhis: Rooted in ancient traditions, Sindhis are known for their deep connection to the Sufi saints and their music. The Indus River flows through Sindh, just as poetry and music flow through the veins of its people.
Pashtuns: From the northwestern region, the Pashtuns are a proud and resilient people, deeply connected to their traditions and the rugged landscape they call home. Their code of hospitality, called Pashtunwali, ensures that guests are treated with the utmost respect.

Baloch: In Balochistan, you'll find a people as rugged and untamed as the land they inhabit. The Baloch are known for their fierce independence and their rich tradition of storytelling and music.

This cultural tapestry is evident in everything—from the clothes people wear to the way they celebrate festivals. When you travel through Pakistan, you're not just visiting different places; you're stepping into different worlds.

Key Attractions: What to Expect

Now that we've set the stage, let's talk about the highlights—those must-see spots that will make your trip to Pakistan unforgettable. Lahore Fort and Badshahi Mosque: These iconic landmarks are the epitome of Mughal architecture. Expect to be awed by the intricate tile work, the grandiose scale, and the history that whispers from every corner.

Hunza Valley: Often described as paradise on earth, Hunza is where you go to disconnect from the world and reconnect with nature. Expect crystal-clear rivers, towering mountains, and some of the friendliest people you'll ever meet.

Mohenjo-Daro: Step back in time as you walk through the ruins of this ancient city. Expect to be fascinated by the advanced urban planning and the mystery that still surrounds this ancient civilization.

Karachi's Clifton Beach: A visit to Karachi isn't complete without a stroll along Clifton Beach. Expect a lively atmosphere with families, vendors, and the endless horizon of the Arabian Sea.

Ranikot Fort: Often called the Great Wall of Sindh, this lesser-known gem is the world's largest fort, yet it remains off the beaten path. Expect to feel like an explorer as you wander its vast, deserted walls.

Insider Tips

Timing Is Everything: Pakistan's climate varies greatly from region to region. The best time to visit the northern areas is during the summer months (May to September), while the south is more pleasant in winter (November to February).
Be Prepared for Surprises: In Pakistan, things don't always go according to plan, but that's part of the charm. Flexibility is your best friend here. Whether it's an impromptu invitation to a wedding or a detour to a hidden shrine, go with the flow.
Learn a Few Phrases: While English is widely understood, knowing a few words in Urdu or the local language will endear you to the locals and enrich your experience.

 Expect to be surprised, challenged, and ultimately, enchanted by this incredible land.
Now, let's begin our journey together.

PART 2

Exploring Pakistan by Provinces

Chapter 2: Punjab - The Heart of Pakistan

Lahore

Lahore, the cultural epicenter of Pakistan, is where history and Lahore, Pakistan's cultural epicenter, merges history and modernity seamlessly. Known as the "City of Gardens," it features a vibrant arts scene and deep historical roots.

Begin your visit at the Lahore Fort and Badshahi Mosque, prime examples of Mughal architecture. In the evening, stroll through the bustling streets of the old city, savoring Lahore's street food. Explore cultural highlights including the Lahore Museum, and the lively bazaars of Anarkali and Shalimar Gardens, where Mughal-era charm remains vibrant.

Faisalabad

Faisalabad, known as the "Manchester of Pakistan," is the industrial hub of Punjab. While it may not have the historical grandeur of Lahore, it offers a different kind of charm. Explore the city's vibrant markets like the Clock Tower Bazaar, and experience its local textile industry. Faisalabad is also a gateway to exploring the region's agricultural richness. Visit the local farms to see the production of cotton and sugarcane up close.

Multan

Multan, the "City of Saints," is steeped in spiritual history and is renowned for its Sufi shrines. The city's mausoleums, such as the Shrine of Bahauddin Zakariya and Shah Rukn-e-Alam, offer an insight into the mystical side of Punjab.

Historical Sites

Badshahi Mosque
The Badshahi Mosque, built in 1673 by Emperor Aurangzeb, stands as one of the largest mosques in the world. Its red sandstone walls and marble inlay work are classic examples of Mughal artistry.

The mosque's grand minarets and expansive courtyards provide a serene space for reflection amidst the bustling city. When visiting, try to catch a sunset; the changing light enhances the mosque's stunning architectural details.

Lahore Fort
The Lahore Fort, a UNESCO World Heritage Site, is a labyrinth of palaces, gardens, and defensive walls.

Key highlights include the Sheesh Mahal, adorned with intricate mirror work, and the Alamgiri Gate, a grand entrance that hints at the fort's historical significance. Guided tours can offer fascinating insights into the fort's history, from the Mughal era to its role under British rule.

Shalimar Gardens
Shalimar Gardens, a masterpiece of Mughal landscape architecture, exemplifies the elegance of Mughal garden design. The terraced gardens, with their cascading fountains and reflective pools, offer a tranquil retreat.
The gardens are a testament to Mughal horticultural prowess and provide a picturesque setting for leisurely walks and contemplative moments.

Cultural Festivals, Cuisine, and Traditions

Festivals
Punjab is a land of vibrant festivals. The Lahore Literary Festival attracts intellectuals and artists from across the country, offering a platform for cultural exchange. Baisakhi, marking the harvest season, is celebrated with traditional dances, music, and feasts.
The Urs of Sufi saints in Multan is a spiritually significant event that draws thousands of devotees, celebrating with devotional music and poetry.

Cuisine
Punjab's cuisine is a feast for the senses. Lahore's street food scene is legendary—don't miss out on the spicy chaats, kebabs, and the rich, buttery naans. The famed Lahore ke Pakore (fried snacks) are a must-try.
Faisalabad offers hearty, traditional fare, including the robust flavors of desi ghee-based dishes. Multan is renowned for its sweets, such as the delicious Multani Sooji (semolina dessert) and Khoya (reduced milk).

Traditions
Punjab's traditions are deeply rooted in its rural and urban cultures. The vibrant dances like Bhangra and Gidda are integral to local celebrations and festivities. Traditional attire, such as the colorful Punjabi kurta and phulkari embroidery, reflects the region's rich cultural heritage. Punjab's hospitality is legendary—expect to be welcomed with warmth and generosity wherever you go.

Chapter 3: Sindh - The Land of Sufis

Major Cities

Karachi
Karachi, Pakistan's bustling metropolis and economic powerhouse, is a city where modernity meets tradition. The cityscape is a mosaic of colonial architecture, contemporary skyscrapers, and vibrant markets. Visit Clifton Beach for a scenic escape and indulge in local seafood delicacies at the waterfront. Karachi's diverse food scene includes dishes from Karachi biryani to spicy kebabs at Burns Road.

Hyderabad
Known for its historical significance and cultural heritage, Hyderabad is famed for its rich Sindhi culture. Explore the bustling markets and taste the famous Hyderabadi biryani.
The city's architectural gems include the Shahbaz Qalandar Shrine and the historic Hyderabad Fort. Hyderabad's culture is deeply rooted in Sufi traditions, making it a center of spiritual and historical exploration.

Sukkur
Sukkur, located on the Indus River, is renowned for its historical and architectural landmarks. The city is home to the iconic Sukkur Barrage, which regulates the flow of the Indus River. Visit the ancient ruins of Bhanbhore and the beautiful Sadh Belo Temple on the Indus. Sukkur's vibrant markets offer a taste of Sindhi craftsmanship and traditional attire.

Historical Sites

Mohenjo-Daro

Mohenjo-Daro, one of the cradles of civilization, is a must-visit for history enthusiasts. The ruins of this ancient city reveal sophisticated urban planning and advanced drainage systems.
Walk through the remnants of the Great Bath and residential areas to understand the scale of this early metropolis. The site is a UNESCO World Heritage Site, offering profound insights into early urban life.

Ranikot Fort

Often called the "Great Wall of Sindh," Ranikot Fort is one of the largest forts in the world. Its expansive walls and strategic location offer panoramic views of the surrounding landscape. The fort's construction spans several eras, including Hindu and Islamic periods, making it a fascinating study in military architecture and historical evolution.

Makli Necropolis

Makli Necropolis, a UNESCO World Heritage Site, is an extensive burial ground dating back to the 14th century. The necropolis is renowned for its intricately designed tombs and mausoleums, showcasing the rich architectural and artistic heritage of Sindh. The elaborate carvings and stunning tile work reflect the grandeur of Sindhi funerary art.
Coastal Life, Sufi Culture, and Regional Cuisine

Coastal Life

Sindh's coastline offers a blend of natural beauty and cultural vibrancy. The beaches of Karachi, like Clifton and Manora, provide a refreshing retreat from the city's hustle.

Explore the fishing villages along the coast to witness traditional maritime practices and sample fresh seafood. The coastal lifestyle reflects a unique blend of simplicity and vibrancy.

Sufi Culture

Sindh is the heartland of Sufi culture in Pakistan. Cities like Hyderabad and Sehwan Sharif are spiritual hubs, with shrines dedicated to Sufi saints like Lal Shahbaz Qalandar.

Attend a qawwali performance at a shrine to experience the soulful music that characterizes Sindhi Sufism. The culture emphasizes mystical devotion, poetry, and music, offering a deep spiritual experience.

Regional Cuisine

Sindhi cuisine is known for its bold flavors and hearty dishes. Karachi's street food scene features spicy kebabs, aromatic biryanis, and various chaats.

Hyderabad's specialties include the flavorful Hyderabadi biryani and Sindhi Karhi, a tangy curry. Sukkur's markets offer a variety of traditional sweets and snacks, showcasing Sindh's culinary diversity.

Local Etiquette: Sindhi culture is deeply respectful of traditions and spirituality. Dress modestly, especially when visiting religious sites, and be mindful of local customs.

Chapter 4: Khyber Pakhtunkhwa - The Frontier Province

Welcome to Khyber Pakhtunkhwa (KP), Pakistan's rugged Frontier Province, where history and culture intertwine with dramatic landscapes. This chapter unveils the essence of KP, from its vibrant cities and ancient sites to its rich tribal heritage.

Major Cities

Peshawar: The cultural heartbeat of KP, Peshawar blends ancient traditions with modern dynamics. Explore the bustling Qissa Khwani Bazaar, renowned for its vibrant market and rich history.
The Peshawar Museum offers a glimpse into the region's past with its impressive collection of Gandharan art. Don't miss the historic Walled City, which showcases the city's centuries-old architecture and traditional Pashto culture.

Abbottabad: Nestled in the foothills of the Himalayas, Abbottabad is renowned for its serene landscapes and pleasant climate. A hub for educational institutions, it's ideal for a peaceful retreat.
Visit the picturesque Shimla Hill for panoramic views, and experience the local Pashto hospitality.

Swat: Often referred to as the "Switzerland of the East," Swat captivates with its stunning natural beauty. The valley's lush green hills and crystal-clear rivers make it a haven for outdoor enthusiasts.
The Buddhist archaeological site at Butkara Stupa provides a fascinating insight into the region's historical significance.

Historical Sites

Bala Hisar Fort: Overlooking Peshawar, this imposing fort stands as a testament to the region's strategic importance. Originally built by the Mughal Empire, it has been a symbol of power and defense through the ages. Explore its battlements and get a feel for its historical significance.

Takht-i-Bahi: A UNESCO World Heritage site, Takht-i-Bahi is an ancient Buddhist monastic complex perched on a hill. Its well-preserved ruins offer a rare glimpse into the Buddhist era, with intricate carvings and a serene atmosphere that transports visitors back in time.

Khyber Pass: This historic mountain pass has been a crucial trade route for centuries. The Khyber Pass is not only a geographical marvel but also a historical gateway that has witnessed numerous invasions and migrations.
The surrounding landscape is as dramatic as its history, offering stunning views and a sense of the pass's strategic importance.

Tribal Culture and Pashto Traditions

KP is home to a diverse range of tribes, each with its unique customs and traditions. The Pashto-speaking tribes are particularly notable for their vibrant cultural practices. Experience traditional Pashto music, dance, and the famed Pashtun hospitality.
Local festivals such as the Jashn-e-Baharan (Spring Festival) showcase traditional attire, folk dances, and culinary delights.

Mountain Adventures

For the adventurous, KP offers a playground of rugged terrains and high peaks. The Swat and Kaghan valleys are ideal for trekking, hiking, and camping.

Explore the serene lakes of Saif-ul-Malook and Bashikou, or venture into the dense forests of Malam Jabba for a thrilling skiing experience. The breathtaking landscapes of KP provide endless opportunities for exploration and adventure.

Chapter 5: Balochistan - The Land of Mysteries

Welcome to Balochistan, a region of enigmatic landscapes and ancient traditions. This chapter uncovers the essence of Balochistan, where each corner tells a story of its own.

Major cities

Quetta: Balochistan's capital and a major trading hub. Quetta is the gateway to the province's diverse attractions. Visit the Quetta Archaeological Museum for insights into local history and culture.

The bustling Liaquat Bazaar offers a taste of local life with its vibrant markets and traditional crafts.

Gwadar: A port city on the Arabian Sea, Gwadar is emerging as a vital economic center.

The Gwadar coastline boasts stunning vistas, including the serene Gwadar Beach and the dramatic Hammerhead Point. The city is also a gateway to explore the natural wonders of the Makran Coastline.

Zhob: Known for its scenic beauty and strategic location, Zhob is an ideal spot for experiencing Balochistan's rugged terrain.

The nearby Ziarat Shrine and the picturesque landscapes of the surrounding mountains make Zhob a charming stop.

Historical and Cultural Sites

Miri Fort: Overlooking the city of Quetta, Miri Fort offers panoramic views and a glimpse into the region's military history. Originally a stronghold, it has witnessed numerous historical events and provides an evocative sense of the past.

Bolan Pass: A historical route through the Sulaiman Mountains, Bolan Pass has served as a major trade and invasion route throughout history. The dramatic landscapes and historical significance of the pass are a must-see for history enthusiasts.

Kalat: The Kalat Fort, a grand structure perched atop a hill, reflects the architectural brilliance of the local Baloch rulers. Explore its ancient walls and learn about its strategic importance in Balochistan's history.

Tribal Culture and Traditions

Balochistan is a land rich in tribal culture and traditional practices. The Baloch people are known for their distinctive Pashto language, traditional music, and vibrant festivals.
Experience the cultural heritage through local events like the Sibi Mela, a traditional fair showcasing folk music, dance, and crafts.

Natural Wonders and Adventures

Hingol National Park: A gem of natural beauty, Hingol National Park offers stunning landscapes ranging from rugged mountains to expansive deserts.

The park is home to the unique Princess of Hope rock formation and the ancient Hinglaj Mata Temple, an important pilgrimage site.

Ratti Gali Lake: Situated in the northern part of Balochistan, Ratti Gali Lake is a high-altitude alpine lake surrounded by snow-capped peaks. It's a serene destination for trekking and camping, offering breathtaking views and a tranquil atmosphere.

Makran Coastal Highway: Drive along this scenic highway to experience the dramatic coastline of Balochistan. The route features striking geological formations, including the spectacular Hingol National Park and the stunning beaches of Gwadar.

Chapter 6: Gilgit-Baltistan - The Mountain Paradise

Welcome to Gilgit-Baltistan, a realm of awe-inspiring peaks and serene beauty. This chapter offers an insider's guide to the stunning landscapes, vibrant culture, and adventure that define this mountainous paradise.

Major Towns and Key Attractions

Gilgit: The administrative hub of Gilgit-Baltistan, Gilgit is your gateway to the region's natural splendor. Visit the Gilgit Viewpoint for panoramic vistas of the surrounding mountains and the confluence of the Gilgit and Hunza Rivers.
The ancient Baltit Fort, with its intricate wooden architecture, provides a glimpse into the region's historical significance.

Skardu: Nestled in the heart of the Karakoram, Skardu is a base for exploring some of the most breathtaking landscapes.
The serene Shangrila Resort, also known as "Lower Kachura Lake," offers a tranquil retreat. Nearby, the ancient Skardu Fort and the mesmerizing Deosai National Park, often called the "Land of Giants," are must-see destinations.

Hunza: Renowned for its stunning scenery and hospitable locals, Hunza is a gem of Gilgit-Baltistan. The majestic Baltit Fort and the panoramic views from Altit Fort offer historical insights and breathtaking landscapes.
For natural beauty, visit Attabad Lake, created by a landslide in 2010, and marvel at its striking turquoise waters.
Iconic Mountains

K2: The second-highest mountain in the world, K2 stands as the crown jewel of the Karakoram Range. Known for its challenging climbs and breathtaking vistas, K2 attracts mountaineers from around the globe. Even if you're not climbing, the Base Camp trek provides awe-inspiring views and a sense of the mountain's grandeur.

Nanga Parbat: The "Killer Mountain," Nanga Parbat is the ninth-highest peak in the world and offers dramatic landscapes and a sense of rugged adventure. Its base camp trek is renowned for its striking views and the stark contrast between the icy peak and the surrounding lush valleys.

Rakaposhi: With its impressive height and beautiful snow-covered peak, Rakaposhi is a prominent feature of the Karakoram Range. It is less frequented than K2 or Nanga Parbat but offers equally stunning vistas and excellent trekking opportunities.

Trekking Routes and Adventures

Fairy Meadows: Named for its ethereal beauty, the Fairy Meadows trek offers unparalleled views of Nanga Parbat.
The trek is relatively moderate and leads you to a lush meadow with spectacular mountain views, ideal for photography and experiencing the region's natural beauty.

Ratti Gali Lake: Located in the southern part of Gilgit-Baltistan, the trek to Ratti Gali Lake is challenging but rewarding. The lake, surrounded by snow-capped peaks, offers a serene and pristine environment.

The Hunza Valley Trek: This trek provides a comprehensive exploration of Hunza, including the historic Baltit and Altit Forts, terraced fields, and picturesque villages. It offers an immersive experience of the local culture and stunning landscapes.

Local Culture and Traditions

Gilgit-Baltistan is rich in cultural diversity, with distinct traditions in each region. The people are known for their hospitality and vibrant festivals. Experience the Shandoor Polo Festival, which showcases traditional polo games and local music. Engage with local artisans to explore traditional crafts, including intricate woodwork and colorful textiles.

Chapter 7: Azad Kashmir - The Valley of Paradise

Welcome to Azad Kashmir, a region where natural beauty meets rich cultural heritage. This chapter provides an insider's guide to the picturesque towns, stunning landscapes, and vibrant Kashmiri traditions that define this enchanting valley.

Major Towns and Key Attractions

Muzaffarabad: The capital of Azad Kashmir, Muzaffarabad serves as the gateway to the region's wonders. Visit the Red Fort (Chak Fort), a historic fortress offering panoramic views of the confluence of the Jhelum and Neelum Rivers. The city's bustling bazaars and local eateries provide a taste of Kashmiri culture and cuisine.

Neelum Valley: Renowned for its breathtaking beauty, Neelum Valley is a must-visit for nature enthusiasts. The valley is dotted with scenic spots like Keran and Shounter Lake. Explore the lush green meadows and tranquil rivers, and take in the serene beauty that defines this region.

Rawalakot: Often referred to as the "Pearl Valley," Rawalakot is known for its pleasant climate and scenic landscapes. The town serves as a base for exploring nearby attractions like Pindi Point and Banjosa Lake. The local markets offer traditional Kashmiri crafts and delicious food.

Natural Attractions
Pir Chinasi: A prominent hilltop offering stunning views of Muzaffarabad and the surrounding valleys.

Pir Chinasi is known for its panoramic vistas and the shrine dedicated to Pir Chinasi, a revered saint. The drive up to the hilltop is as scenic as the views from the top.

Banjosa Lake: Situated near Rawalakot, Banjosa Lake is an artificial reservoir surrounded by beautifully landscaped gardens. The lake's tranquil waters and the surrounding scenery make it a popular spot for picnics and leisurely boat rides.

A high-altitude alpine lake located in the Neelum Valley, Ratti Gali Lake is a hidden gem. Its crystal-clear waters, surrounded by snow-capped peaks, create a serene environment perfect for trekking and nature photography. The trek to the lake offers panoramic views of the surrounding mountains.

Kashmiri Culture and Crafts

Azad Kashmir's cultural richness is reflected in its vibrant traditions and craftsmanship. The Kashmiri people are known for their hospitality and artistry.
Explore the local markets in Muzaffarabad and Rawalakot to discover traditional Kashmiri shawls, rugs, and intricate wood carvings.

Kashmiri cuisine is a highlight, with dishes such as Rogan Josh and Yakhni showcasing the region's culinary heritage.

Attend local festivals and fairs to experience traditional music, dance, and cultural performances.

PART 3

Major Cities of Pakistan

Chapter 8: Karachi - The City of Lights

Karachi, Pakistan's bustling metropolis and economic powerhouse. This chapter unveils the vibrant urban life, historical landmarks, and coastal attractions that define this dynamic city.

Port City Vibes: Karachi is Pakistan's largest city and a key commercial hub. Its diverse neighborhoods reflect a blend of cultures and histories. The cityscape ranges from sleek skyscrapers in Clifton to the traditional markets of Saddar. Karachi's urban pulse is evident in its bustling streets and energetic vibe.

Quaid-e-Azam's Mausoleum: This iconic white marble mausoleum is the final resting place of Muhammad Ali Jinnah, Pakistan's founder. Its grand architecture and serene surrounding gardens make it a must-visit for anyone interested in Pakistan's history.

Frere Hall: Built during the British colonial era, this elegant building with its Gothic architecture now hosts art exhibitions and literary events. The adjoining gardens provide a pleasant retreat from the city's hustle.

Clifton Beach: Popular for its lively atmosphere, Clifton Beach offers a picturesque coastline with various recreational activities. Enjoy camel rides or simply take in the sea breeze while strolling along the promenade.

Manora Island: A short ferry ride from Karachi, Manora Island is known for its historic lighthouse and tranquil beaches. The island provides a refreshing escape from the city's bustle.

Culinary Diversity: Karachi's food scene is a vibrant tapestry of flavors reflecting its multicultural makeup. From spicy street food to high-end dining, the city offers something for every palate.

Street Food: Explore the bustling lanes of Saddar and Karachi's famous Burns Road for delectable street food. Try the spicy Nihari (slow-cooked meat stew), savory Kebabs, and Karachi's renowned Bun Kebab (burger).

Vibrant Nightlife: Karachi's nightlife is as diverse as its population. From lively nightclubs to casual lounges, the city offers a range of options.

Club Scene: For a high-energy experience, head to clubs like The Cosa Nostra or The Chatterbox. These venues offer a mix of live music, DJ sets, and a chic atmosphere.

Cultural Events: Enjoy live performances, theater, and music festivals at venues like the Karachi Arts Council and the National Academy of Performing Arts (NAPA).

Bustling Markets: Karachi's markets are a shopper's paradise, offering everything from traditional crafts to modern fashion.

Zainab Market: Famous for its handicrafts, textiles, and jewelry, Zainab Market is the go-to place for unique souvenirs and traditional items.

Dolmen Mall: For a contemporary shopping experience, visit Dolmen Mall in Clifton. This upscale mall features international brands, dining options, and entertainment facilities.

Interesting Trivia

Economic Hub: Karachi contributes approximately 30% of Pakistan's GDP and serves as the country's financial and commercial center.

Cultural Melting Pot: The city is home to diverse communities, including Sindhis, Punjabis, Baloch, and various ethnic groups from across Pakistan and beyond.

Chapter 9: Lahore - The Cultural Capital

Lahore, the heart of Pakistan's cultural heritage and a city where history, art, and life converge.

Historical Landmarks and Mughal Architecture

Badshahi Mosque: One of the largest mosques in the world, the Badshahi Mosque stands as a testament to Mughal grandeur. Its imposing red sandstone structure, intricate marble inlays, and vast courtyard are awe-inspiring.
Visiting this iconic site at sunset is particularly magical, as the fading light casts a golden hue over the mosque's domes.

Lahore Fort: Adjacent to the Badshahi Mosque, Lahore Fort (Shahi Qila) is a UNESCO World Heritage site that showcases the opulence of the Mughal era.
Explore the Sheesh Mahal (Palace of Mirrors) and the stunning Alamgiri Gate. The fort's mix of Persian and Mughal architecture offers a fascinating glimpse into the region's history.

Shalimar Gardens: Built by Emperor Shah Jahan, the Shalimar Gardens are a masterpiece of Mughal landscape design. The gardens' terraced layout, flowing fountains, and symmetrical beauty make it an oasis of calm amidst the city's hustle. A stroll through these gardens offers a serene retreat, perfect for reflecting on the city's historical grandeur.

Festivals and Vibrant Street Life

Basant Festival: Lahore's spring festival, Basant, is a celebration of life and color. The sky fills with vibrant kites, and the city buzzes with excitement. Though kite-flying is the highlight, Basant is also marked by music, dance, and traditional food.

The festival embodies Lahore's joyous spirit and love for celebration.

Walled City: The old city, with its narrow alleys and bustling bazaars, is the beating heart of Lahore's street life.
Anarkali Bazaar, one of Asia's oldest markets, is a treasure trove of traditional crafts, jewelry, and textiles. Wander through the Walled City to experience Lahore's vibrant street culture and rich history up close.

Food Streets: Lahore is synonymous with food, and its streets are alive with culinary delights. The Gawalmandi Food Street is a must-visit, offering a range of traditional Lahori dishes. From spicy Nihari to mouth-watering Golgappas, the flavors here are bold and unforgettable. The food streets of Lahore are where the city's love for food truly comes to life.

Lawrence Gardens (Bagh-e-Jinnah): A lush, green haven in the city, Lawrence Gardens are perfect for a leisurely walk or a peaceful afternoon. With its beautifully manicured lawns, ancient trees, and colonial-era buildings, this garden is a reminder of Lahore's diverse historical influences.

Race Course Park: Another green escape, Race Course Park is known for its serene environment and well-maintained walking tracks. It's a popular spot for morning joggers and families, offering a quiet retreat from the city's bustling streets.

Interesting Trivia

Cultural Hub: Lahore is known as the cultural capital of Pakistan, hosting numerous literary festivals, art exhibitions, and music events throughout the year.

City of Gardens: Lahore is often referred to as the "City of Gardens" due to its numerous parks and green spaces, a legacy of its Mughal and colonial past.

Chapter 10: Islamabad - The Modern Capital

Islamabad, Pakistan's meticulously planned capital, stands as a symbol of modernity blended seamlessly with nature. This chapter delves into the city's urban planning, modern architecture, and the natural beauty that frames this diplomatic hub.

Urban Planning and Modern Architecture

Masterpiece of Planning: Designed in the 1960s by Greek architect Constantinos Apostolou Doxiadis, Islamabad's layout reflects modern urban planning principles.
The city is divided into sectors, each with its own amenities, creating a sense of order and efficiency. This thoughtful design makes Islamabad unique among South Asian capitals, offering a balanced mix of residential, commercial, and green spaces.
Faisal Mosque: The most iconic structure in Islamabad, Faisal Mosque, is a marvel of modern architecture. Its geometric design, devoid of traditional domes, is both futuristic and reverent.
Nestled against the backdrop of the Margalla Hills, the mosque's towering minarets and expansive prayer hall embody the intersection of contemporary design and Islamic tradition.

Pakistan Monument: This flower-shaped monument symbolizes the unity of Pakistan's diverse cultures. Its petal-like structure represents the four provinces and three territories. The inner walls of the monument are adorned with intricate murals depicting significant events in Pakistan's history, making it not only an architectural wonder but also a cultural landmark.

Natural Beauty and Nearby Attractions

Margalla Hills National Park: Islamabad's green lungs, the Margalla Hills, offer a tranquil escape within the city.
The park's trails range from easy walks to challenging hikes, with each path providing stunning views of the city below. Daman-e-Koh, a popular viewpoint, is particularly striking at dusk when the city lights begin to twinkle.

Rawal Lake: A serene spot for relaxation, Rawal Lake is surrounded by beautifully landscaped gardens and picnic spots. Boating and fishing are popular activities here, making it a perfect retreat from the urban environment. The lake's calm waters and the surrounding greenery provide a peaceful setting for both locals and visitors.

Shakarparian Park: Overlooking Islamabad, Shakarparian Park offers a mix of cultural and natural attractions. The Pakistan Monument Museum, located here, provides insights into the country's history, while the park itself is ideal for leisurely strolls, with panoramic views of the city and the Margalla Hills.

Diplomatic Hubs and Cultural Centers

Diplomatic Enclave: As the seat of Pakistan's government and home to numerous embassies, Islamabad is the country's diplomatic center. The Diplomatic Enclave is a secure area where embassies from around the world are located, reflecting the city's importance on the global stage.

Lok Virsa Museum: Islamabad's cultural heartbeat can be felt at the Lok Virsa Museum. This cultural center showcases the rich heritage of Pakistan's various regions through art, music, and crafts. It's an essential visit for those interested in understanding the cultural diversity that makes up Pakistan.

Saidpur Village: A blend of the old and the new, Saidpur Village offers a glimpse into the region's rural past while being surrounded by modern Islamabad. The village's restored buildings, traditional eateries, and handicraft shops provide a charming contrast to the city's modernity.

Interesting Trivia

Highest Literacy Rate: Islamabad boasts one of the highest literacy rates in Pakistan, reflecting its status as a center of education and governance.

Green City: With its abundance of parks and tree-lined streets, Islamabad is often referred to as one of the greenest capitals in the world.

Chapter 11: Peshawar - The Gateway to Central Asia

Peshawar, one of South Asia's oldest cities, stands as a living testament to history. As the gateway to Central Asia, it's a city where ancient traditions and vibrant culture coexist. This chapter provides an insider's look into Peshawar's historical significance, bustling bazaars, formidable forts, and the rich tapestry of Pashtun culture.

Historical Significance

Crossroads of Empires: Peshawar's strategic location made it a key player in the histories of empires, from the Persian Achaemenid Empire to the Mughal Dynasty. This city, known as Purushapura in ancient times, has seen the rise and fall of civilizations, leaving behind a wealth of historical landmarks. Every corner of Peshawar tells a story, whether it's the Buddhist stupas that once dotted the landscape or the Mughal architecture that still stands.

Bala Hisar Fort: A symbol of Peshawar's resilient spirit, Bala Hisar Fort has been a witness to the city's turbulent past. This fort, originally built by the Mughal Emperor Babur, offers panoramic views of Peshawar. The fort's thick walls and towering bastions speak of its strategic importance, while the view from the top provides a sense of the city's expanse and its historical layers.

Qissa Khwani Bazaar: Known as the "Bazaar of Storytellers," Qissa Khwani is where history comes alive. In the past, travelers would gather here to exchange stories over cups of green tea. Today, it remains a vibrant market where you can find everything from traditional Pashtun clothing to aromatic spices.

The bazaar is also home to ancient havelis, their wooden balconies overlooking the bustling streets below.

Khyber Pass: Just beyond Peshawar lies the fabled Khyber Pass, a route that has seen countless invaders, traders, and travelers. The pass, with its rugged terrain and steep cliffs, has long been the gateway between the Indian subcontinent and Central Asia. Visiting the Khyber Pass is not just a journey through stunning landscapes; it's a passage through the annals of history.

Pashtunwali: The code of life for the Pashtuns, Pashtunwali, emphasizes hospitality, honor, and courage. In Peshawar, you'll witness this code in action. The city's hospitality is legendary, with every home opening its doors to guests. The honor-bound traditions of Pashtunwali are reflected in the city's way of life, where respect and loyalty are paramount.

Cuisine: Peshawar's cuisine is a flavorful blend of Central Asian and South Asian influences. Rich, aromatic dishes like chapli kebabs and kabuli pulao are staples, often served with freshly baked naan. The city's food scene, centered around its vibrant markets and roadside eateries, offers a culinary journey that is both hearty and satisfying.

Traditional Attire: The traditional Pashtun dress, shalwar kameez, is worn with pride in Peshawar. Men often sport the pakol, a woolen cap, while women's clothing features intricate embroidery. The city's tailors are renowned for their craftsmanship, creating garments that are both traditional and timeless.

Interesting Trivia

Cultural Melting Pot: Peshawar's unique location has made it a melting pot of cultures, where South Asian, Central Asian, and Persian influences converge.

Cinema Culture: Peshawar has a rich cinema history, being the hometown of Bollywood legends like Dilip Kumar and Raj Kapoor.

PART 4

Nature & Adventure

Chapter 12: The Majestic Mountains of Pakistan

Pakistan's towering peaks are among the most magnificent in the world, drawing adventurers and nature lovers alike. This chapter delves into the key mountain ranges—Himalayas, Karakoram, and Hindu Kush—and explores the thrilling experiences that await in these rugged terrains.

Key Mountain Ranges

Himalayas: The Himalayas, often called the "Abode of Snow," stretch across the northern regions, offering a breathtaking landscape of towering peaks and serene valleys. In Pakistan, this range includes some of the world's highest and most challenging mountains, including Nanga Parbat, known as the "Killer Mountain.
" The Himalayan range is not just about the high-altitude drama; it's also home to lush valleys like Kaghan and Swat, where nature's beauty is on full display.

Karakoram: The Karakoram Range, home to K2, the second-highest peak in the world, is a mountaineer's dream. This range is characterized by its stark, rugged beauty—an expanse of rock and ice that challenges even the most seasoned climbers.
The Karakoram is also home to some of the most renowned trekking routes, like the Baltoro Glacier trek, which offers unparalleled views of the towering Trango Towers and Broad Peak.

Hindu Kush: The Hindu Kush, a lesser-known but equally dramatic range, forms the western boundary of the mountainous north.

This range is steeped in history, having served as a route for ancient traders and invaders.

Its peaks may not rival those of the Karakoram in height, but they offer an untamed, raw beauty that is perfect for those seeking solitude and adventure off the beaten path.

Trekking and Mountaineering

Baltoro Glacier Trek: This trek is one of the most challenging and rewarding in the world, taking you deep into the heart of the Karakoram Range.

The journey begins in the town of Skardu and follows the Baltoro Glacier, a massive river of ice, leading to the base of K2. Along the way, you'll pass iconic formations like the Cathedral Towers and witness the sheer verticality of the Karakoram peaks.

Fairy Meadows and Nanga Parbat Base Camp: For those looking for a less grueling but equally stunning adventure, Fairy Meadows offers a surreal experience. Located at the base of Nanga Parbat, this lush alpine meadow lives up to its name with its tranquil beauty.

The trek to the base camp of Nanga Parbat is a moderate one, rewarding trekkers with close-up views of the majestic peak and the Raikot Glacier.

Adventure Sports: The mountainous regions of Pakistan are a playground for adventure sports enthusiasts. From high-altitude skiing in the Karakoram to white-water rafting in the rivers that cut through these ranges, there's no shortage of adrenaline-pumping activities.

For climbers, the peaks of the Karakoram and Hindu Kush offer some of the most technical and challenging climbs in the world, drawing elite mountaineers year after year.

Interesting Trivia

K2's Unique Shape: K2, known as the "Savage Mountain," is often considered the most difficult mountain to climb due to its steep slopes and unpredictable weather. Its unique pyramidal shape has become an iconic symbol of mountaineering challenges.

The Great Trango Tower: Part of the Karakoram Range, the Great Trango Tower is famous for having the greatest nearly vertical drop on Earth, making it a coveted destination for the world's top rock climbers.

Chapter 13: The Rivers and Lakes of Pakistan

Pakistan's rivers and lakes are the lifeblood of its diverse landscape, offering both natural beauty and a wealth of activities. Here's a guide to experiencing these majestic waters.

The Indus: The Soul of Pakistan
The Indus River is not just a river; it's a legend. Flowing from the Tibetan plateau into the Arabian Sea, the Indus has nurtured civilizations for millennia. For the traveler, it offers mesmerizing views and a chance to connect with the country's ancient past. River rafting in the northern stretches provides an adrenaline rush against a backdrop of stunning landscapes.

Trivia: The Indus is one of the longest rivers in the world, stretching over 3,180 kilometers.

Jhelum: The Serene Waterway
Jhelum River, with its gentle flow, mirrors the calm beauty of the regions it passes through. Known for its historical significance, particularly in the battles of Alexander the Great, Jhelum today is a serene spot for fishing enthusiasts. The riverbanks are perfect for a peaceful retreat.

Chenab: The River of Romance
The Chenab River has inspired poets and lovers alike. Flowing through the Punjab plains, this river is closely linked with the folklore of Heer and Ranjha. Its banks are ideal for leisurely picnics, while boating on the Chenab offers a tranquil experience, with vast fields stretching into the horizon.

Saiful Muluk: The Fairy Tale Lake

Nestled in the Kaghan Valley, Lake Saiful Muluk is a place straight out of a fairy tale. Surrounded by snow-capped peaks, the lake is famous for its enchanting reflections and is a favorite among trekkers. Local legend says that fairies come down to dance on its shores during the night.

Attabad: A Lake Born of Tragedy

Attabad Lake, formed after a massive landslide in 2010, has become one of Pakistan's most striking tourist destinations. Its turquoise waters are a stark contrast to the rugged Karakoram Range. Kayaking, boating, and fishing are popular here, making it a must-visit for adventurers.

Manchar: Asia's Largest

Manchar Lake, near Dadu in Sindh, is Asia's largest freshwater lake. This vast expanse of water is not only a hub for fishing but also a sanctuary for migratory birds. The floating village on the lake offers a unique glimpse into the lives of the Mohana tribe.

River Rafting and Fishing: A Call to Adventure

Pakistan's rivers are prime locations for rafting, especially in the northern areas. The Gilgit and Swat rivers offer thrilling rapids for those seeking adventure. Fishing, on the other hand, is a more relaxed way to enjoy the natural beauty, with the trout-filled rivers of Khyber Pakhtunkhwa being particularly popular.

Boating: A Scenic Escape

Whether it's a peaceful boat ride on the Jhelum or a thrilling speedboat race on the Indus, Pakistan's rivers and lakes provide ample opportunities for boating enthusiasts. The calm waters of Lake Saiful Muluk are perfect for a paddle boat ride, offering serene views of the surrounding mountains.

Pakistan's rivers and lakes are more than just bodies of water—they are stories etched into the landscape. Each offers a unique experience, from the ancient currents of the Indus to the serene beauty of Saiful Muluk. Whether you seek adventure or tranquility, these waters will leave you spellbound.

Chapter 14: The Deserts of Pakistan

Pakistan's deserts are vast, enigmatic landscapes that hold a wealth of cultural and natural wonders. From the expansive Thar to the lesser-known Kharan, these deserts offer a journey into the heart of the country's arid beauty.

Thar: The Vibrant Desert

The Thar Desert, stretching across Sindh and into Rajasthan, is a landscape alive with color and culture. Here, the golden sands are punctuated by vibrant villages, where local traditions thrive.

Expect to witness lively cultural festivals like the Thar Desert Festival, where music, dance, and camel races bring the desert to life. The Thar is also home to unique wildlife, including the elusive Indian gazelle and the desert fox.

Trivia: The Thar Desert is one of the most densely populated deserts in the world, with people living in small, colorful villages.

Cholistan: The Land of Lost Forts

Cholistan Desert, located in Punjab, is not just about endless sand dunes; it's a place steeped in history. The ruins of Derawar Fort, an imposing structure that rises from the desert, tell tales of a bygone era. Cholistan is also famous for its annual jeep rally, which draws adventure seekers from around the world.
The desert's cultural festivals, like the Cholistan Desert Festival, offer a glimpse into the rich heritage of the region, with traditional crafts and music.

Kharan: The Mysterious Wilderness
Kharan Desert in Balochistan is a landscape of stark beauty, where the sand meets the rugged mountains. Known for its harsh climate and remote location, Kharan is less frequented but offers a serene escape for those looking to explore uncharted territories.

This desert is also home to unique wildlife, including the Kharan viper and various bird species. The silence of Kharan is profound, offering an experience of solitude and reflection.

Desert Safaris: A Journey into the Sands
Desert safaris in Pakistan are an adventure like no other. In the Thar, camel safaris are a traditional way to explore the dunes, while jeep safaris in Cholistan offer a thrilling ride through the vast desert.

These safaris provide an opportunity to experience the raw beauty of the desert, with stops at historic sites and traditional villages.

Cultural Festivals: Celebrating the Desert Spirit
Each desert in Pakistan has its unique festivals that celebrate the spirit of the region. The Thar Desert Festival is a vibrant showcase of Sindhi culture, while the Cholistan Desert Festival highlights the traditions of Punjab.
These festivals are marked by music, dance, and traditional sports, offering a deep dive into the local culture.

Wildlife: Life in the Sands

Despite the harsh conditions, Pakistan's deserts are teeming with life. The Thar is home to various species of reptiles and mammals, while the Cholistan supports a variety of birdlife, including migratory species.

In Kharan, the sparse vegetation supports unique fauna, making these deserts a haven for wildlife enthusiasts.

The deserts of Pakistan are not merely barren landscapes; they are places of vibrant culture, history, and natural beauty.
Whether you are exploring the lively Thar, the historic Cholistan, or the remote Kharan, these deserts offer an experience of adventure and discovery that is uniquely Pakistani.

PART 5

Cultural Heritage & Traditions

Chapter 15: Pakistan's Great Monuments

Pakistan is home to some of the most significant monuments in the subcontinent, each reflecting the diverse history, architectural genius, and cultural richness of the region. Beyond the more well-known sites, several other monuments carry the stories of empires, resistance, and religious devotion that have shaped the country.

Badshahi Mosque: The Grand Mughal Marvel
Located in Lahore, the Badshahi Mosque is one of the largest mosques in the world and a prime example of Mughal architecture. Commissioned by Emperor Aurangzeb in 1671, the mosque is renowned for its grandeur, with massive minarets, an expansive courtyard, and exquisite marble inlay work. The mosque was also used as a garrison by the British, adding layers to its historical significance.

Insider's Tip: Visit during the late afternoon to witness the mosque's red sandstone glowing in the setting sun, creating an awe-inspiring atmosphere.

Shalimar Gardens: Mughal Splendor in Bloom
A UNESCO World Heritage site, the Shalimar Gardens in Lahore were laid out in 1641 by Emperor Shah Jahan. These gardens are a classic representation of the Mughal love for nature and symmetry, with terraced levels, water cascades, and intricately carved marble pavilions. The gardens were designed not just as a leisure space but also as a symbol of paradise on earth.

Trivia: The Shalimar Gardens were once the site of royal gatherings, where poetry, music, and dance would celebrate the opulence of the Mughal court.

Ranikot Fort: The Great Wall of Sindh

Ranikot Fort, located in Sindh, is often referred to as the "Great Wall of Sindh" and is one of the largest forts in the world. The origins of the fort are shrouded in mystery, but it is believed to have been constructed by the Talpur dynasty in the 17th century. The fort's massive walls stretch over 32 kilometers, enclosing a complex network of military architecture.

Insider's Tip: The fort is best explored during the cooler months, and the sunset view from its ramparts is nothing short of breathtaking.

Makli Necropolis: The City of Silence

Situated in Thatta, Sindh, the Makli Necropolis is one of the largest funerary sites in the world, spanning over 10 square kilometers. The site is home to tombs and monuments dating back to the 14th century, showcasing a blend of Islamic, Persian, and Hindu architectural styles. The intricately carved stonework on these tombs narrates stories of the rulers, saints, and scholars buried here.

Trivia: The Makli Necropolis is a UNESCO World Heritage site and is often referred to as the "City of Silence" due to its eerie, yet serene atmosphere.

Derawar Fort: The Desert Sentinel

Standing tall in the Cholistan Desert, Derawar Fort is a striking example of desert architecture. The fort's 40 bastions can be seen for miles across the barren landscape, and its origins date back to the 9th century. However, the fort was rebuilt by the Nawabs of Bahawalpur in the 18th century and served as their stronghold.

Insider's Tip: The fort is accessible by a challenging desert drive, but the journey is worth it for the panoramic views and the sense of stepping back in time.

Katas Raj Temples: A Hindu Pilgrimage Site

The Katas Raj Temples, located in the Salt Range of Punjab, are a complex of ancient Hindu temples that date back to the 6th century. The temples are built around a sacred pond, which is said to have formed from the tears of Shiva after the death of his wife, Sati. These temples are a testament to the region's religious diversity and ancient architectural styles.

Trivia: The Katas Raj complex was not only a religious site but also a center of learning, where scholars from across the subcontinent would gather.

Takht-i-Bahi: A Glimpse into Buddhist Gandhara

Takht-i-Bahi, near Mardan in Khyber Pakhtunkhwa, is one of the most well-preserved Buddhist monastic complexes in the world. Dating back to the 1st century, this site offers a fascinating insight into the Gandhara civilization, with its stupas, courtyards, and meditation cells still intact. The site is perched on a hill, offering sweeping views of the surrounding plains.

Insider's Tip: Visit in the early morning to avoid the heat and enjoy the tranquil atmosphere that once inspired Buddhist monks.

Noor Mahal: The Palace of Lights
Built in 1872 by Nawab Sadiq Muhammad Khan IV in Bahawalpur, Noor Mahal is an exquisite example of Italian architecture with Islamic influences. The palace was constructed as a residence but was soon abandoned due to superstitions.

Trivia: The palace's design reflects a blend of Western and Islamic architectural styles.

Faisalabad Clock Tower: The Symbol of Colonial Legacy
The Clock Tower in Faisalabad, constructed in 1903, is a colonial-era landmark that symbolizes British architectural influence in Pakistan. The tower, part of a larger marketplace, features a classic clock and is surrounded by vibrant bazaars.

Insider's Tip: The area around the Clock Tower is ideal for experiencing local market life and traditional street food.

Rohtas Fort: The Fortress of Resistance
Built in the 16th century by the Afghan king Sher Shah Suri, Rohtas Fort is located near Jhelum.
It was constructed to suppress the Gakhar tribes and stands as a formidable example of military architecture, with its massive walls, bastions, and intricate gateways.
Trivia: The fort's design reflects a blend of Persian and Indian architectural influences, intended to intimidate rather than accommodate.

Wazir Khan Mosque: A Masterpiece of Mughal Art
Situated in Lahore, the Wazir Khan Mosque, built in 1634, is celebrated for its intricate tile work and frescoes. It was commissioned by Wazir Khan, the governor of Lahore under Emperor Shah Jahan, and is known for its ornate decorative elements.

Insider's Tip: The mosque's vibrant tile work and calligraphy are best appreciated up close, so take your time exploring its inner courtyards.

Chaukhandi Tombs: The Necropolis of the Talpurs
Located near Karachi, the Chaukhandi Tombs date back to the 15th century and serve as the burial site for the Talpur dynasty. The tombs are known for their elaborate carvings and unique architectural style, which combines Islamic and local influences.

Trivia: The tombs' intricate stone carvings and detailed patterns reflect the Talpur's status and artistry.

The Minar-e-Pakistan: The Birthplace of a Nation
Standing proudly in Iqbal Park, Lahore, the Minar-e-Pakistan commemorates the Lahore Resolution of 1940, which laid the foundation for the creation of Pakistan. Designed by the architect Naseer-ud-Din Murat, this tower symbolizes the country's struggle for independence.
Insider's Tip: Visit early in the morning to avoid crowds and enjoy the expansive park surrounding the monument.

Chapter 16: Festivals and Celebrations

Pakistan's festivals reflect its rich cultural tapestry and diverse heritage. From grand national celebrations to vibrant regional events, each festival offers unique insights into local traditions and communal joy.

Eid ul-Fitr: The Festival of Breaking the Fast
Eid ul-Fitr marks the end of Ramadan, the holy month of fasting. This festival is celebrated with immense joy and festivity across Pakistan.

Homes and streets are adorned with lights, and families come together for feasts featuring dishes like biryani, kebabs, and sweets such as sheer khurma. The sight of new clothes and the sounds of celebratory prayers mark the day.

Insider's Tip: Visit local markets in the days leading up to Eid to experience the vibrant atmosphere of shopping and preparations. Trivia: The festival often includes charity distributions, where individuals and families provide Zakat al-Fitr (charitable donations) to help the less fortunate.

Eid ul-Adha: The Festival of Sacrifice
Eid ul-Adha, or Bakra Eid, commemorates the willingness of Ibrahim (Abraham) to sacrifice his son as an act of obedience to God. Celebrations involve the ritual sacrifice of livestock such as sheep, goats, and cows. Families divide the meat among themselves, their neighbors, and the poor, reinforcing communal bonds and generosity.
Insider's Tip: Observe the local traditions of sacrifice and distribution in rural areas for a more authentic experience.

Trivia: The festival is marked by grand feasts and special prayers at mosques, with many people wearing new clothes and participating in festive gatherings.

Basant: The Festival of Kites

Basant, held in Lahore and other cities, celebrates the arrival of spring with a spectacular display of kites. This vibrant festival is characterized by colorful kites filling the skies, traditional music, and street food. It's a time when families and friends gather on rooftops and open spaces to enjoy the kite-flying competitions.

Insider's Tip: Join the locals on rooftops during Basant to fully appreciate the festival's energetic atmosphere and kite-flying spirit. Trivia: The festival also features traditional foods like saffron rice and chicken kebabs, and is an opportunity to experience the lively folk music of the region.

Independence Day: A Celebration of Freedom

Observed on August 14th, Independence Day marks Pakistan's independence from British rule in 1947. The day is celebrated with patriotic fervor, including flag hoisting ceremonies, parades, and cultural performances. Major cities like Islamabad and Karachi host grand fireworks displays, while schools and government buildings are decorated with the national flag.

Insider's Tip: Attend the flag hoisting ceremony at the Quaid-e-Azam's Mausoleum in Karachi or the official celebrations in Islamabad for a patriotic experience.

Trivia: Independence Day also includes special broadcasts on television and radio, featuring national songs and historical documentaries.

Sindh Festival: A Celebration of Sindhi Culture
The Sindh Festival celebrates the rich cultural heritage of the Sindh province. Held annually in Karachi and other major cities, it showcases Sindhi music, dance, arts, and crafts. The festival also includes traditional Sindhi cuisine, vibrant clothing, and historical exhibitions. Insider's Tip: Explore the craft stalls and cultural performances to experience the diversity and richness of Sindhi traditions.

Trivia: The festival aims to promote Sindhi culture and heritage, providing insights into the region's historical and artistic legacy.

Shandur Polo Festival: The Highest Polo Ground
Held annually in the Shandur Pass, the Shandur Polo Festival features polo matches on the world's highest polo ground, situated at 3,700 meters above sea level. The festival, held in July, includes traditional music, dance performances, and cultural displays from the Chitral and Gilgit-Baltistan regions.

Insider's Tip: Attend the festival for a unique high-altitude polo experience and explore the local culture of the high mountain communities.

Trivia: The festival is known for its unique polo rules, where players often ride bareback and use traditional polo sticks.

Kalash Festivals: Celebrations of the Kalash People
The Kalash community in Chitral celebrates several unique festivals, including Chilam Joshi (spring festival), Uchau (harvest festival), and Phool (flower festival).

These events feature traditional Kalash dances, music, and rituals, offering a rare glimpse into their ancient pagan culture.

Insider's Tip: Participate in these festivals to experience the vibrant cultural practices and traditions of the Kalash people, known for their distinct customs and attire.

Trivia: The Kalash festivals are deeply rooted in agricultural and seasonal cycles, reflecting the community's close relationship with nature.

Cultural and Religious Processions: Regional Significance
Across Pakistan, various cultural and religious processions mark significant occasions.
These include the procession of Muharram in Shia communities, and local fairs and festivals celebrating regional saints and historical figures.

Insider's Tip: Attend these processions with respect and curiosity to gain insight into local religious practices and community life.

Trivia: These processions often involve elaborate rituals, traditional music, and public gatherings that reflect the deep spiritual and communal bonds of the regions.

Chapter 17: The Diverse Cuisine of Pakistan

Pakistan's cuisine is a rich tapestry of regional flavors and culinary traditions, reflecting the country's diverse culture and history. From spicy street food to elaborate feasts, each province offers unique gastronomic experiences.

Punjab: The Heart of Punjabi Cuisine
Punjab is renowned for its hearty and flavorful dishes. The cuisine is characterized by the use of rich spices, ghee, and robust flavors.

Signature dishes include:
Butter Chicken (Murgh Makhani): A creamy, spiced chicken curry, made with a tomato and butter-based sauce.
Sarson da Saag and Makki di Roti: A traditional combination of mustard greens curry with cornbread, celebrated for its earthy flavors and rustic charm.

Insider's Tip: Visit local dhabas (roadside eateries) for authentic Punjabi flavors, particularly in cities like Lahore and Amritsar.

Trivia: Punjab's culinary heritage is deeply influenced by both Mughal and regional agricultural practices, resulting in rich, diverse dishes.

Sindh: Coastal and Spicy Delights
Sindhi cuisine features a blend of spicy, tangy, and aromatic dishes, influenced by its coastal geography and historical trade routes.
Sindhi Biryani: A spicy rice dish with marinated meat, potatoes, and a tangy yogurt base, known for its bold flavors.

Sindhi Karhi: A unique curry made with gram flour dumplings and vegetables, flavored with tamarind and turmeric.

Insider's Tip: Try local seafood dishes in Karachi, which is famed for its fresh fish and vibrant flavors.

Trivia: Sindhi cuisine often incorporates a variety of spices and herbs, reflecting the region's historical trading connections.

Khyber Pakhtunkhwa: Flavorful Pashtun Fare
Khyber Pakhtunkhwa's cuisine is influenced by Pashtun traditions, featuring simple yet flavorful dishes with a focus on grilled meats and bread.

Chapli Kebab: Spiced minced meat kebabs, known for their aromatic spices and crispy texture.

Pulao: A fragrant rice dish often cooked with meat and spices, distinguishing itself from biryani by its subtler flavors.

Insider's Tip: Visit Peshawar's historic eateries to experience traditional Pashtun meals, often served with freshly baked naan.

Trivia: Pashtun cuisine places a strong emphasis on grilling and kebabs, with influences from Central Asian and Afghan culinary traditions.

Balochistan: Rich and Robust Flavors

Balochistan's cuisine is hearty and robust, characterized by its use of spices and slow-cooked meats.

Sajji: Whole stuffed chicken or lamb, marinated and slow-roasted, known for its deep, savory flavors.

Kaak: Traditional Balochi bread, often served with meat dishes, highlighting the region's emphasis on simplicity and flavor.

Insider's Tip: Experience Balochi dishes in Quetta, where traditional methods of cooking and unique spices are used.

Trivia: Balochi cuisine often includes slow-cooking methods and large portions, reflecting the region's nomadic heritage and agricultural practices.

Street Food Across Pakistan

Pakistan's street food scene is vibrant and diverse, offering a variety of quick bites that capture the essence of local flavors.

Chaat: A popular street food across cities, featuring a mix of chickpeas, potatoes, yogurt, and tangy tamarind chutney.

Gol Gappa (Pani Puri): Crisp puris filled with spicy tamarind water, chickpeas, and potatoes, a favorite in bustling street markets.

Insider's Tip: Explore local street food vendors to experience authentic, regional snacks. Karachi and Lahore are particularly renowned for their diverse street food offerings.

Trivia: Street food in Pakistan often varies from region to region, reflecting local tastes and traditions.

Famous Restaurants and Culinary Spots

Several restaurants and culinary destinations are celebrated for their exceptional dining experiences:

Monal (Islamabad): Offers a panoramic view of the city along with a wide range of traditional and contemporary dishes.

Café Zouk (Karachi): Known for its fusion of Pakistani and international cuisines, it's a popular spot for diverse culinary experiences.

Cooco's Den (Lahore): A historical restaurant that combines traditional Lahori dishes with a rich cultural atmosphere.

Insider's Tip: For a refined dining experience, seek out restaurants that showcase regional specialties and offer insights into local culinary traditions.

Trivia: Many renowned restaurants in Pakistan are celebrated for their unique decor and ambiance, reflecting the rich cultural heritage of their regions.

Pakistan's diverse cuisine is a journey through its regional traditions and flavors. Each dish tells a story of cultural fusion, historical influences, and local practices, offering a unique culinary adventure for every palate.

Chapter 18: Arts and Crafts of Pakistan

Pakistan's arts and crafts are a vibrant reflection of its rich cultural heritage, showcasing a blend of traditional techniques and contemporary expressions. From intricate textiles to dynamic performances, each form offers a glimpse into the country's diverse artistic landscape.

Traditional Crafts

Truck Art

A striking form of folk art, truck art transforms ordinary vehicles into mobile canvases. Characterized by its bold colors, intricate patterns, and elaborate designs, it's a celebration of local aesthetics and creativity.

Features: Floral motifs, geometric patterns, and vivid, multi-colored depictions of daily life and folklore.

Insider's Tip: Explore Karachi's busy roads to see some of the most elaborate truck art in action. Local artists often add personalized touches, making each truck unique.

Trivia: Pakistani truck art has gained international recognition, symbolizing the country's vibrant culture and artistic flair.

Pottery

Pakistan's pottery traditions date back thousands of years, reflecting regional styles and techniques.

Multan Pottery: Known for its blue and white ceramic tiles, often featuring intricate geometric patterns.

Chiniot Pottery: Renowned for its red clay pottery with distinctive hand-painted designs.

Insider's Tip: Visit local bazaars in Multan and Chiniot for authentic pottery pieces. Each piece tells a story through its design and craftsmanship.

Trivia: The art of pottery in Pakistan has been influenced by Persian and Central Asian techniques, resulting in unique, region-specific styles.

Carpets
Handwoven carpets are a testament to Pakistan's rich textile heritage, particularly from the regions of Peshawar and Lahore.

Peshawar Carpets: Famous for their intricate designs and high-quality wool, often featuring traditional patterns like medallions and floral motifs.

Lahore Carpets: Known for their fine craftsmanship and vibrant colors, reflecting a mix of Mughal and Persian influences.

Insider's Tip: Explore carpet emporiums in Peshawar and Lahore to find exquisite handmade carpets. Look for carpets that feature traditional patterns and high-quality craftsmanship.

Trivia: Pakistani carpets are often crafted using age-old techniques passed down through generations, preserving traditional weaving methods.

Music and Dance

Classical Music

Pakistan's classical music tradition encompasses various genres, including:

Qawwali: A devotional music genre popularized by legends like Nusrat Fateh Ali Khan. It features Sufi poetry and is known for its ecstatic and soulful performance.

Raga Music: Traditional Indian classical music forms practiced in Pakistan, including ragas performed on instruments like the sitar and tabla.

Insider's Tip: Attend a live Qawwali performance in Lahore or Karachi to experience the spiritual and musical intensity of this genre.

Trivia: Qawwali has roots in the Sufi tradition and has been instrumental in popularizing South Asian music globally.

Folk Dance

Folk dances vary widely across Pakistan's regions, each reflecting local traditions and cultural narratives.

Balochi Dance: Characterized by energetic movements and colorful costumes, often performed at festivals and weddings.

Punjabi Bhangra: A vibrant and dynamic dance associated with harvest celebrations, featuring lively beats and rhythmic movements.

Insider's Tip: Witness folk dance performances during local festivals or cultural events to see authentic expressions of regional traditions.

Trivia: Traditional dances often involve elaborate costumes and are performed during significant cultural and religious events.

Literature

Classical Literature
Pakistan's literary heritage is deeply rooted in classical Urdu and Persian literature.

Poetry: Works of poets like Mirza Ghalib and Faiz Ahmed Faiz continue to influence contemporary literature with their profound expressions of love, politics, and social issues.

Prose: Writers such as Saadat Hasan Manto and Ahmed Nadeem Qasmi have contributed significantly to modern Urdu literature, exploring complex social themes.

Insider's Tip: Explore literary festivals and bookshops in cities like Lahore and Karachi to engage with contemporary and classic works of Pakistani literature.

Trivia: Urdu literature often blends classical and modern influences, reflecting the rich linguistic and cultural diversity of the region.

Contemporary Art

Pakistan's contemporary art scene is flourishing, with artists gaining recognition both locally and internationally.

Modern Painting: Artists like Shahzia Sikander and Imran Qureshi are known for their innovative approaches, merging traditional motifs with modern techniques.

Sculpture and Installation Art: Contemporary sculptors are exploring new forms and materials, reflecting on social and political themes.

Insider's Tip: Visit galleries and art festivals in Karachi and Lahore to experience cutting-edge contemporary art.

Trivia: Contemporary Pakistani artists are increasingly gaining international acclaim, showcasing the country's dynamic and evolving artistic landscape.

Pakistan's arts and crafts offer a deep dive into its cultural soul, showcasing a blend of traditional skills and contemporary creativity. From vibrant truck art to soulful music and dynamic literature, each form provides a unique window into the country's diverse and rich heritage.

PART 6

Travel Tips & Insights

Chapter 19: Practical Travel Information

Visa Requirements

Navigating visa requirements for Pakistan requires a clear understanding of regulations. Here's what you need to know:

Tourist Visas: Most travelers need a visa to enter Pakistan. The process involves applying through the nearest Pakistani embassy or consulate. Some countries may qualify for an e-visa, which simplifies the procedure.

Business Visas: For business purposes, a formal invitation from a Pakistani company is usually required. This visa often allows for a longer stay compared to tourist visas.

Visa on Arrival: Certain nationalities can obtain a visa on arrival, but it's essential to check specific eligibility criteria and ensure all documents are in order.

Insider's Tip: Always check the latest visa requirements before traveling, as regulations can change. Ensure your passport is valid for at least six months beyond your planned stay.

Trivia: The visa application process for Pakistan can sometimes involve additional documentation, such as proof of accommodation and financial stability.

Transportation

Getting around Pakistan efficiently requires an understanding of local transport options:

Domestic Flights: Major cities like Karachi, Lahore, and Islamabad are well-connected by domestic flights. Airlines like PIA offer frequent services.

Trains: The Pakistan Railways network connects various regions, providing a scenic and economical way to travel. For long distances, consider booking a sleeper class for comfort.

Buses: Intercity buses are a popular choice for traveling between major towns and cities. Look for reputable operators like Daewoo Express for a reliable experience.

Local Transport: Within cities, options include ride-sharing apps like Careem and Uber, local taxis, and rickshaws. For a more local experience, try the traditional tongas or horse-drawn carriages.

Insider's Tip: Traffic congestion can be significant in major cities, so plan your travel times accordingly. Ride-sharing apps often offer a safer and more transparent alternative to local taxis.

Trivia: Pakistan's railway system is one of the oldest in South Asia, with some routes dating back to the British colonial period.

Accommodation

Pakistan offers a wide range of accommodation options catering to various budgets and preferences:

Luxury Hotels: High-end hotels like the Pearl Continental and Serena Hotels offer world-class amenities and are found in major cities.

Mid-Range: There are numerous comfortable and affordable hotels and guesthouses in urban and rural areas. Chains like Best Western provide reliable options.

Budget Stays: Hostels and budget guesthouses are available in popular tourist spots. Websites like Booking.com and Airbnb offer insights and reviews to help you choose.

Insider's Tip: Book accommodations in advance, especially during peak travel seasons and major festivals. Look for places with good reviews for a reliable stay.

Trivia: Many high-end hotels in Pakistan offer traditional hospitality, including local cuisine and cultural performances.

Safety Tips

Ensuring safety during your travels is paramount. Here's how to stay secure:

Travel Advisories: Stay updated on travel advisories from your government. Regions experiencing political unrest or natural disasters may have specific safety warnings.

Local Laws: Familiarize yourself with local laws and customs. Pakistan has strict regulations regarding dress codes, especially for women, and drug offenses.

Emergency Contacts: Keep emergency contact numbers handy, including local police and your country's embassy or consulate.

Insider's Tip: Avoid large gatherings and be cautious of your surroundings in busy markets and public places. Register with your embassy for added safety if you're staying for an extended period.

Trivia: Pakistan's security situation can vary greatly by region, so it's important to tailor your precautions based on the areas you plan to visit.

Local Etiquette

Understanding local customs enhances your travel experience:

Dress Code: Dress conservatively, especially in rural areas and religious sites. Women should wear long dresses or skirts and cover their heads in some areas.

Social Norms: Greetings are often formal, with a handshake or a nod. It's polite to remove shoes when entering someone's home or a mosque.

Dining Etiquette: It's customary to eat with the right hand. Be mindful of traditional dining practices and respect local customs.

Health Advice

Staying healthy during your trip involves some basic precautions:
Vaccinations: Ensure you're up-to-date on routine vaccinations. Hepatitis A and B, typhoid, and tetanus are recommended for travelers to Pakistan.
Food and Water Safety: Avoid consuming tap water and street food unless you're confident of its cleanliness. Stick to bottled water and well-cooked food.
Travel Insurance: Obtain comprehensive travel insurance that covers medical emergencies and trip cancellations.

Trivia: Pakistan has a diverse climate, so pack appropriate clothing for the weather conditions and your planned activities.

Pakistan offers a dynamic and rich travel experience, and understanding practical aspects can make your journey smoother. From visa requirements to local customs, being well-prepared ensures a more enjoyable and safe exploration of this vibrant country.

Chapter 20: Off the Beaten Path - Hidden Gems of Pakistan

Shigar Fort, Gilgit-Baltistan

This restored 17th-century fort, now a luxurious heritage hotel, offers an immersive experience into the ancient Baltistan culture. Its intricate wooden carvings and serene setting by the Shigar River make it a captivating stop for history enthusiasts and those seeking tranquility.

Insider's Tip: Explore the nearby Shigar Valley for stunning landscapes and traditional Baltistani architecture. The area is ideal for hiking and offers breathtaking views of the Karakoram Range.

Trivia: Shigar Fort was originally built as a royal residence for the rulers of Baltistan and is a prime example of traditional Kashmiri architecture.

Kalash Valleys, Khyber Pakhtunkhwa

Nestled in the Chitral district, the Kalash Valleys are home to the Kalash people, known for their distinct polytheistic culture and vibrant festivals. Visit during the Chilam Joshi festival in May for an immersive experience of Kalash traditions, music, and dance.

Insider's Tip: Be respectful of local customs and traditions. The Kalash people are known for their hospitality but appreciate travelers who are mindful of their unique cultural practices.

Trivia: The Kalash community's origins are shrouded in mystery, with some theories suggesting they are descendants of Alexander the Great's troops.

Hingol National Park, Balochistan

This expansive park features diverse landscapes, from striking rock formations to ancient river valleys. The Fairy Meadows and the Mud Volcanoes are notable highlights. The park is a haven for adventure seekers, offering opportunities for off-road exploration and wildlife spotting.

Insider's Tip: Bring sufficient supplies, as facilities in the park are minimal. The best time to visit is between October and March when temperatures are more manageable.

Trivia: Hingol National Park is home to the largest mud volcano in Pakistan, which creates a dramatic and unique landscape.

Remote Villages
Ratti Gali, Azad Kashmir

A remote alpine village nestled in the Himalayas, Ratti Gali offers stunning views and a chance to experience the simplicity of rural life. The area is known for its pristine lake and is perfect for trekking and camping.

Insider's Tip: Reach Ratti Gali by a guided trek, as the area is not easily accessible by public transportation. Pack light and be prepared for changing weather conditions.

Trivia: Ratti Gali Lake is a glacial lake and is often covered in snow, even in summer, adding to the picturesque beauty of the region.

Chitral, Khyber Pakhtunkhwa

This remote town is the gateway to the Upper Chitral region and offers an authentic experience of mountain life. Explore the vibrant Chitrali culture, visit the ancient Chitral Fort, and enjoy the local hospitality. Insider's Tip: Engage with local guides to explore the surrounding valleys, such as the Bumburet Valley, known for its lush greenery and traditional Kalash festivals.

Trivia: Chitral is famous for its unique local breed of goat, the Chitrali goat, known for its distinctively curved horns.

Unique Experiences

Skardu's Deosai Plains, Gilgit-Baltistan

Known as the "Land of Giants," Deosai Plains is a high-altitude plateau that boasts unique wildlife and dramatic landscapes. The plains are renowned for their beautiful wildflower blooms in summer and are perfect for camping and wildlife photography.

Insider's Tip: Acclimatize to the altitude before heading to Deosai. The best time to visit is from June to September when the weather is milder and the plains are covered in wildflowers.

Trivia: Deosai is home to the Himalayan brown bear, one of the rarest bear species, and offers exceptional opportunities for wildlife enthusiasts.

Lal Suhanra National Park, Punjab
This lesser-known park features a mix of desert and wetland ecosystems, providing a haven for birdwatchers and nature lovers. The park is known for its diverse bird species and scenic beauty, with a variety of flora and fauna.

Insider's Tip: Visit during the winter months for the best birdwatching experience, as migratory birds flock to the park during this time.

Trivia: Lal Suhanra is one of Pakistan's largest national parks and was established to conserve the unique desert and wetland ecosystems of the region.

Tips for Adventurous Travelers and Cultural Explorers

Plan Ahead: For remote locations, research thoroughly and plan your itinerary in advance. Local guides are often essential for navigating less-traveled paths and ensuring safety.

Respect Local Cultures: Be mindful of cultural norms and practices, especially in traditional or religious communities. Always seek permission before taking photographs.

Prepare for the Unexpected: Pack appropriate gear for various weather conditions and terrains. Carry essentials like water, food, and first-aid supplies, as amenities may be limited in remote areas.

Stay Connected: Although many hidden gems are off the beaten path, maintaining communication with local contacts or guides is crucial for safety and navigation.

Trivia: Exploring Pakistan's hidden gems often involves traversing diverse landscapes, from lush valleys to arid deserts, each offering a unique glimpse into the country's rich cultural and natural heritage.

Conclusion

Embarking on a journey through Pakistan is like unlocking a treasure chest of diverse experiences, each more captivating than the last.

From the majestic heights of the Himalayas and Karakoram to the serene lakes and rugged deserts, every region reveals its own story and character. Whether you're tracing the footprints of ancient civilizations at hidden forts or savoring the vibrant pulse of local festivals, Pakistan invites you to witness its untold beauty and rich cultural tapestry.

As you explore this multifaceted country, you'll find that every corner holds a new adventure, a fresh perspective, and a deep connection to a heritage that spans millennia. The bustling streets of Lahore, the tranquil valleys of Gilgit-Baltistan, and the remote charm of Chitral each offer unique insights into the spirit of Pakistan. Engage with its people, embrace its traditions, and let the land itself guide your journey.

So pack your bags, open your mind, and set out to discover Pakistan's hidden gems. The experiences you gather and the stories you collect will not only enrich your travels but also leave you with memories that linger long after your journey ends. Pakistan awaits—each path you tread is a chapter in your own epic adventure.

As you turn the final page of this guide, remember: the real magic of travel lies in the moments of connection, discovery, and wonder. Here's to your extraordinary adventure in Pakistan—where every journey is a story, and every story is an invitation to explore deeper.

Printed in Great Britain
by Amazon